The Young Widow's Guide
to Grieving and Raising
Children Alone

IT TAKES
COURAGE

Dr. Roneisa Matero

NEW YORK

LONDON • NASHVILLE • MELBOURNE • VANCOUVER

It Takes Courage

The Young Widow's Guide to Grieving and Raising Children Alone

Published in New York, New York, by Morgan James Publishing in partnership with Difference Press. Morgan James is a trademark of Morgan James, LLC. www.MorganJamesPublishing.com

ISBN 9781642796605 paperback
ISBN 9781642796612 eBook
ISBN 9781642796995 audioBook
Library of Congress Control Number: 2019943889

Cover & Interior Design by:
Christopher Kirk
www.GFSstudio.com

Morgan James is a proud partner of Habitat for Humanity Peninsula and Greater Williamsburg. Partners in building since 2006.

Get involved today! Visit
MorganJamesPublishing.com/giving-back

It Takes Courage

This book is dedicated to my late husband Christopher Alan Matero, both of my amazing children Brianna and Dante, my parents Ronny and Judy Nicholson, my best friend Steve, and my friends, family, military personnel, and Chris' teammates.

Without my husband giving the ultimate sacrifice for our country I would not have experienced the grief journey, nor would I have been given the most important job I have ever had and that was raising my children to be the amazing, loving, caring, smart adults they are today.

Without my children I would not be the person I am today. They have taught me as much about grieving and being strong as anyone. They are both some of the strongest people I know. They have endured what I feel is one of the hardest life lessons and that is the lesson of dealing with loss and death. Not just any loss, but the death of their father at such a young age. I commend them for their bravery and courage to keep going and to never give up on their dreams.

To my loving and supportive parents, I would not be the person I am today without your love and guidance throughout my life and especially when Chris died. You were there for me through all the ups and downs and twists and turns of my grief journey. And you still are and for that I am eternally grateful.

To Steve, you have been a tremendous pillar of support for me throughout this process. Thank you for pushing me to finish what I start to keep going when I wanted to quit and for loving me anyway.

And to all my family, friends, and the military personnel and Chris' teammates who have helped and loved me along the way, I want to thank you for listening when I needed to vent, being there when I needed to cry, and not judging me when I made mistakes along my grief journey.

Table of Contents

It Takes Courage

*"The healing power of even the most microscopic
exchange with someone who knows in a
Flash precisely what you are talking about
because she experienced that thing too
cannot be overestimated"*
– Cheryl Strayed

L et me start off by saying that if you are reading this book, I commend you. You are courageous and strong, and you are willing to do what it takes to be a good parent and raise your children in the face of loss and grief. This is one of the most challenging and exhausting tasks you will ever take on.

I remember when I sat down to tell my children that their daddy wasn't coming home. I was not prepared for the questions that followed and I felt like I had failed them in some way. Grief is a normal response to loss, but I believe for young widows with children, the loss is intensified and on a much larger scale. We not only have to deal with our own grief, but we are now responsible for helping our children along their grief journeys as well. Children, much like adults, grieve in their own unique ways. As mothers we want to protect our children and keep them safe from harm. Helping them deal with the feelings and emotions of grief can seem like a daunting task and makes us feel helpless at times.

Each person's grief journey is unique, yet the process of grief is similar. In this book we will discuss the grief related to losing a spouse. That, in my opinion, is the most painful and long-lasting type of grief one can experience. This type of grief/loss changes every little detail of your life and your children's lives forever. Pulling ourselves out of the grips of grief takes courage, commitment, confidence, and determination. There is no right way to deal with grief and people deal with grief differently. It is important not to bury your grief or avoid it. The specific feelings of grief will vary from person to person and with each phase of the grief process.

I have struggled with feelings of inadequacy, fear, anger, sadness, guilt, and shame (to name a few) throughout the years since my husband died suddenly in August of 2002 and I was left with a seven-year-old and five-year-old to raise by myself. But through all the tears, good and bad days, accomplishments, mistakes, trials, and tribulations I am still here, and my children are grown and married. I now have two amazing grandchildren who I get to see grow up and I thank God every day that I chose to stay in this fight and move forward through my grief all those years ago when I thought my life was over.

Through my C.O.U.R.A.G.E process, which I outline in this book, you will learn how to be ready for the feelings, emotions, and phases of grief when they come and able to face them head on as you move through each one and see the sun on the other side of the storm. Your children are depending on you to be there and be strong and courageous as you go along life's path of grief, while simultaneously carrying them and helping them along their own grief journeys. You have been given the most important job God has asked you to do, and that is to show up and be courageous for yourself and your children and raise them by yourself.

My prayer is that this book will bring a sense of understanding and give you hope as you face the worst chapter or season of your life, living, grieving, and raising children. As young widows raising children, we face a unique challenge that only we can identify with. Being a single mom has its own set of challenges, but adding the overwhelming, unpredictably debilitating, pain of grief makes this already-important job of raising children that much more difficult. Promise me you won't give up. You've got this. You are not alone in your journey. Don't live your life in grief and sadness! Learn to carry the grief and live forward.

CHAPTER 1

My Story

*"What we have once enjoyed we can
never lose. All that we love deeply
becomes a part of us."*
– Helen Keller

As I think back, with tears streaming down my face, on the day that forever changed my life, I am forever thankful and grateful for the love I shared with my husband, Chris. Even though our time together was too short (and it always is), I am humbled to be able to share my story with you in hopes that I may give you a glimmer of hope to help you as you and your children move along your own grief journeys.

My journey has not been easy. I will start at the beginning. I left my small-town home in Southeast Oklahoma at the tender age of eighteen, shortly after high school, to join the Air Force with a guaranteed job as a flight medic. You see, I had always dreamed of growing up to be a doctor someday. My parents worked hard their whole lives, but they could not afford for me to go to college. So, I decided to join the military to travel the world and to get my education. I dreamed as a child about traveling to other countries and seeing other parts of the world. I had never been to more than four states: Oklahoma, Texas, Arkansas, and Louisiana. In August of 1990, I got on an airplane for the first time in Oklahoma City to go to basic training at Lackland Air Force Base in San Antonio, Texas. I completed basic training and the flight medic school and was stationed at Little Rock Air Force Base (AFB) in Arkansas in spring of 1991. I worked in the flight surgeon's office on base and was assigned to a squadron on flight status. That meant I would deploy on temporary duty assignments with my squadron when needed to support the mission. Little Rock was only three hours from where my family lived, so I could go home for frequent visits. That was good, since I was close to my family.

I wanted to travel, and I got my chance when I was deployed to England in early 1993 for three months with my squadron. I was deployed again later that year in the fall of 1993, this time to Saudi Arabia in support of the Gulf War. Shortly before being deployed to Saudi Arabia I was introduced to Chris by one of his teammates. I went out with him one time before my deployment. We wrote back and forth while I was deployed. To my surprise, when our squadron arrived back home, he was waiting for me to get off the plane.

You might say the rest is history. We got married in July 1994, had our first child, Brianna, in January 1995, I left the Air Force and was accepted in the Bachelor of Science registered nurse (RN) program in May 1995. I finished my RN in May 1997 and our second child, Dante, was born in July 1997. We also moved from Little Rock to Pope Air Force Base in Fayetteville, North Carolina in July, just two weeks after Dante was born. I got a job as an RN at the local hospital in Fayetteville working nights on the weekends. When you are a new nurse you take whatever job you can get to gain experience. It was not the ideal situation, but we made it work. Chris had taken an instructor position at the Combat Control School at Pope AFB.

In August of 1998 I returned to college at Duke University to pursue my master's degree in nursing as a Family Nurse Practitioner. I'm not sure why, but I had a strong desire to get that degree. Mind you, it was a two-hour drive back and forth and I had a one-year-old and three-year-old at home, as well as a husband who was in special forces. What was I thinking? Maybe God and the universe knew that I would be raising my children and I needed a career that afforded me the income to support them fully. Personally, I think so.

It amazes me what we can accomplish when we put our minds to it and have God and the universe on our sides. I completed the Family Nurse Practitioner program at Duke in May 2000, by the grace of God, in spite of my major struggles with the commute, my babies at home, and Chris's job. I was so happy that I had finally completed my education and I could now treat patients and own my own clinic doing what I had always wanted to do. Now that I had finished my degree, Chris decided to get off active duty status to complete his criminal justice degree, become an officer, and be home more with me and the kids so that we could have a normal family life. He transferred from active duty to the Air National Guard unit in Kentucky. We moved to Louisville, Kentucky in June 2001 with the dream of finally being settled in one place to raise our children.

Little did I know that the horrendous events that happened in September 2001 would in some way change my life forever. After 9/11, Chris, being in special forces as a Combat Controller, was deployed to Afghanistan from November 2001 until March 2002. Chris arrived back home in April and we bought our dream home together, but unfortunately, with the war still in full swing, he was soon needed once again to protect our borders and our country. He was happy to do this, and was deployed again in April 2002. This time he had a choice of going back to Afghanistan or going to Puerto Rico. We chose Puerto Rico thinking it would be safer and that the kids and I could come to visit him. In May, I moved into our new home with the kids. The guys at the squadron helped me move since Chris was deployed. I worked hard to get the house ready for Chris's return in August.

The first week of July I flew to Puerto Rico to see Chris for our eighth anniversary, July second. We celebrated our anniversary and had an amazing time being together. We stayed at a beautiful hotel on the beach and hung out by the pool, did some sight-seeing around San Juan, and took long walks on the beach every night. As I look back now it was probably the best four days we had spent together. I regret not bringing the kids with me to visit, but at the time I had no idea it would be the last time I would ever see him. He was scheduled to come home at the end of August, after all.

On August 8, 2002, at 0800 in the morning my life would forever be changed. As I was getting ready for work, Brianna and Dante came running upstairs and said, "Mommy, Mommy, there are some guys from Daddy's work here." I racked my brain trying to remember if the guys from the squadron were supposed to come to the house to help me. The Combat Controller team was very close and when part of the team was deployed, the other members of the team would help take care of their family's needs, such as yard work, while they were away. But I could not think of a reason for them to be there that morning.

As I walked to the top of the stairs and looked down at the front door, I could see several men standing on my porch in dress blues. Now, if anyone knows from watching movies about military notification when someone dies – well, this was the scene that I was in the middle of, and my heart sank by the time I got to the bottom of the stairs.

As I opened the door to greet them, they all put their heads down. I said, "I know you are not here to tell me what I think you are here to tell me." They all looked up at me and I knew at that moment I felt like I was in a dream – or rather, a nightmare! It is hard to describe the feelings I had at that moment. Pain, anger, fear, and sadness come to mind. I invited them into the house. I felt like I was going to throw up. My chest was hurting, like my heart had just been ripped out, and I couldn't take a deep breath. One of the men proceeded to tell me that the plane that Chris had been on the night before during a mission had lost contact sometime around 10 p.m. They went on to say that search crews were currently looking for the plane in the area around where they lost the signal. They could not tell me anything for sure, since he was in Puerto Rico. The Puerto Rican military and other members of Chris's team had been searching throughout the night, but the weather was bad and they had to call off the search until the weather cleared. *What? How could they call off the search when my husband and others were missing?* They assured me that there were people searching the area as we spoke. They did confirm that Chris's name was on the manifest roster of who was to be on the flight.

All the men left except one, Jon Rosa, one of Chris's friends and fellow Combat Controllers. He was assigned to help me and my children through this tragic time. He was amazing, kind, and he put up with me yelling, and crying, and praying that God would bring Chris home alive.

Later that day it was determined that the plane that Chris was on had crashed into a mountain around 10 p.m. August 7th and that was why they had lost radar contact. I was later told that the heavy rains and storm had interfered with the instruments of the plane; by the time the obstacle warning light came on it was too late and, as the pilot pulled the plane up, the tail caught the top of the mountain and they crashed. There were some confirmed identities with fingerprints, but all ten passengers onboard were presumed dead. The massive crash of the Hercules C-130 cargo plane had broken it into several pieces and some of the bodies were mangled to the point where there were no fingers to take fingerprints and no teeth for dental record identification. Chris's body was one of the ones so badly damaged that they had to run DNA to confirm his death.

One of Chris's teammates had found his backpack and identified his body by a tattoo on his leg. But we still had to wait for DNA for a positive match identification to know without a doubt that it was Chris. After three days (the time it takes to run DNA), the chaplain, along with two of Chris's team members, returned to my house to tell me that they had found the bodies of all ten military personnel on board the airplane and had confirmed the DNA and identity of the passengers. Yes, my husband, Technical Sgt. Christopher Alan Matero, was on the plane and was confirmed dead.

The reality set in that Chris was not coming home. As you can imagine, that was one of the worst days of my life and still is. I was left with a seven- and five-year-old to raise. I was devastated and felt like my heart had just been ripped out of my chest. I sat down with my children and told them that their daddy was not coming home and that he had gone back to heaven to be with Jesus. They began to cry and so did I. I just sat and held them for what seemed like eternity, but in reality, only a few minutes passed. I realized then that I had been given the biggest challenge and most important job of my life – to raise these two precious children that God had given us by myself.

The first few months were a blur. I was in shock and disbelief. We had the memorial service at the Special Tactics squadron in Louisville for Chris and two of his teammates who were also on the plane. I had to make a decision about where to bury him, but we had never talked about that because after all we were in our twenties with two small children. We had our whole lives ahead of us, or so we thought. I had the choice to bury Chris in Arlington Cemetery, but if I did when would the kids and I get to visit him? Instead I decided to bury him beside his mother in New York. At least we could visit his grave when we would go visit his family, and his dad could go visit him anytime he wanted too.

About six months after Chris's death, I was still in a fog and crying every day. I found myself in my bedroom closet, sitting on the floor reading some old letters he had written to me from Afghanistan and Puerto Rico that year and crying again, of course. I was startled by Brianna and Dante as they opened the closet door and said, "Mommy, are you okay? We know that you love Daddy and miss him, but Mommy, please don't cry anymore." It was then that I decided to stop grieving, or at least stop grieving so openly in front of my children. They became my focus and priority – not that they hadn't been my focus and priority, because they were (after all, they were the reason I was still here and living). It was at that moment that I realized that I had to be strong and courageous for my children, because they were looking to me for support and love to help them deal with the loss of their father.

You see, I didn't know how to grieve or how to deal with the emotions that plagued me every minute of every day. The waves of grief came so often and stayed so long that I felt like I was drowning and couldn't function. Looking back now, I had gone into what I call survival mode and I was so focused on providing the best life for my children that I never stopped long enough to deal with my emotions. I used working as my coping mechanism to get through each day. For me, if I was working and providing the best for my children and helping others, I felt good inside, like I was making a difference. I would work extra shifts and change my plans to work whenever anyone needed me to fill in so I could give my children everything they wanted and needed. I felt like I had to give them the best of everything because they had lost their father. I somehow felt that if I overcompensated for the loss, it would make it better. We had a beautiful four thousand square-foot home and a ten-acre farm with dogs, cats, goats, and horses. The kids had cars and all the best clothes and material things that I could buy. Brianna barrel raced, so I bought a truck and horse trailer and hauled her all over Texas to barrel races. Dante loved motorcycles, so at the age of sixteen, I got him a motorcycle. I took them on vacations every year to wherever they wanted to go. I thought I was doing everything I could to be a great parent and give my children a great life. I worked so hard to provide and give them the best life I could possibly give them, to try and make up for what they had lost.

What I didn't realize as I was working so much was that all they really needed was me. They needed me to be present and love them unconditionally. Yes, I loved them more than anything in this world, but I was working so much and gone from home twelve to fourteen hours a day in the emergency room, I wasn't there as much as I needed to be throughout the years.

Why am I telling you this? I am telling you this because I want you to make different choices if possible while raising your children. I look back now and wish that I had kept a smaller house, worked less outside the home, and spent more time with my children as they grew up.

In the summer of 2016, when my youngest son Dante got married and left home, I realized that I had not let myself fully grieve through the years after Chris died because I had not wanted to upset my children by showing my emotions. I had suppressed all those emotions and when Dante left home and I felt like I had lost the last thing I had with Chris, I went through a major depressive episode. That is what started my journey to find myself again. I felt lost and I didn't know who I was anymore. I had defined myself as a widow and single parent. I suddenly felt empty and alone. I had lost everything I had that connected me to Chris, including my children. Now what?

That is why I decided to write this book. I have felt the desire to write a book since Chris died all those years ago. I've wanted to somehow use my story and grief journey to help other young widows who are struggling and raising children alone. I want this book to provide some hope and encouragement for you as you struggle through your grief journey and raise your children. We all make mistakes and none of us are perfect. Remember, there is no set-in-stone way to grieve. We all grieve in our own way and in our own time. Today I am doing so much better. I have learned to meditate, to listen to my body and my intuition. I feel Chris's presence, and I know he is with me in my heart, though I am still on a healing journey and I will be for the rest of my life. The only difference now is that I have learned through my trials and tribulations to feel through the emotions of grief and, using the techniques I share with you in this book, I have pulled myself out of the depths of depression and I am now grieving in a healthy way. Learning to live again through your grief takes courage. I want you to find strength through my C.O.U.R.A.G.E. process and move forward, raising your children and living and grieving in a healthy way. You can find joy and happiness again.

CHAPTER 2

Stages of Grief

*"It takes strength to make your way through grief,
to grab hold of life and let it pull you forward."*
– Patti Davis

Grief is a natural response to loss. It is nature's way of healing a broken heart. It's the emotional suffering you feel when something or someone you love is taken away. The more significant the loss, the more intense your grief will be. Grief is not a problem to be solved – it is a consequence of our life experience to be carried with us and dealt with daily. As you begin your own journey of living with the loss of a spouse, you will be faced with feelings and emotions that you may have never experienced before. Just remember that almost anything that you experience in the early stages of grief is normal – including feeling like you're going crazy, feeling like you're in a bad dream that you can't wake up from, or questioning your religious or spiritual beliefs. Some common questions we ask in the face of grief are things like, "Why me?" "How am I going to go on without him?," and "How am I going to raise our children by myself?"

According to many experts, grief is measured in stages. Most people refer to the five stages of grief described by Elisabeth Kübler-Ross in her book *On Death and Dying* in 1969. These five stages of grief include denial, anger, bargaining, depression, and acceptance. Now, I am not saying we don't go through all these stages during our grief journey, because we do go through each of these stages and for some people they may come in this order. But there is no end to grief and the emotions felt in these stages will come and go in no particular order throughout your life. The truth is everyone will grieve a loss at some point in their life. Is one of our lessons in life to learn how to grieve? I have often pondered this question through the years and along my grief journey. I will talk about the stages more as we move through the process of grieving in the chapters that follow.

There is no timetable for grieving. Some may grieve faster than others, but we all grieve in some way for the rest of our lives. There is no right or wrong way to grieve. When people are shown the five stages of grief described above, they believe they will happen in that order. They tend to criticize themselves when they feel like they are not grieving right or when they feel like they should be past one stage by a certain time and they are not. Not everyone goes through all five stages, and contrary to popular belief you do not have to go through all the stages in order to heal. There are responses to loss that many people have, but there is not a typical response to loss, as there is no typical loss. Our grieving is as individual as each of our lives. I am here to tell you that I am still grieving the loss of my husband and I feel that I always will in some way or another.

I don't think of grieving as stages to go through, I think of the grieving process like trying to navigate an unknown future that comes in waves that we don't expect. The emotions of grief start out rougher in the beginning. The lows may be deeper and longer at times. Just like grief, in the beginning, the lows can feel like an unrelenting/unforgiving pain that will never end. But as time goes on, the lows become shorter and less intense, just as the difficult times in our lives should become less intense and shorter as time goes by. It takes time to grieve and work through the stages and deal with the intense "real, raw" emotions as they come. There will be times when you feel like you have gotten past the grief, like you are moving forward in life, but a special event such as a family wedding or birth of a child will trigger those emotions and you will experience a strong sense of grief again.

There are many metaphors for describing grief and how we feel while going through the emotions and turmoil that come and go along the journey. But one description of the grief process I heard has stuck with me and I want to share it with you. It goes something like this. Imagine you are sitting in a lounge chair on a beautiful beach sipping an umbrella drink in the soft, warm sun, when suddenly a tidal wave comes and crashes down on you and at that moment your life is changed forever and your heart is broken in a million pieces. You try to get out of the water, but you are continually being swept away into the raging, unforgiving ocean as each wave comes in and goes out. With each wave, grief comes, and you are getting hit from all angles, one after the other. You struggle and try to get to shore and to safety, but the waves are too strong and they keep pulling you back down. You can't breathe because you are just trying to keep your head above water, and you can't eat or sleep because you are trying so hard to keep your head above the water with all the immense pain and grief coming at you with each wave. If you have children who are grieving with you, you are struggling to hold onto your children and desperately trying to keep them above water with each wave of grief that comes.

As a widow, mom, and single parent, you must be prepared to deal with your grief as well as your children's' grief and move forward to healing along the way. The grief process can be exhausting and at times you may feel like you are never going to get through the storm of emotions that come. You may feel like you must carry the weight of your children's' grief on your shoulders and like it is your responsibility that they cope and get through the waves of grief too. As we go along our grief journey, we must be willing to own our own feelings, not suppress them. We must see them for what they are and feel them. We must be present in the pain.

It's okay to cry. In fact, some experts say that crying is the ultimate healer because it is one way the body has of releasing the pain inside. It is thought that as tears flow out of our bodies, so do built-up emotions and pain, letting the body and heart slowly heal with every tear shed. I have often wondered how I still have tears to cry – I have cried so many, I don't know how I could possibly have any left. We must recognize the emotions that come in grief, and feel those emotions, in order to be able to heal and move forward. As you feel and express your feelings during the different phases of your grief, remember: it is not that you are having a bad day, but a grieving day. Just as you cannot stop the waves in the ocean, you cannot stop the feelings of grief. You can only ride the wave of your grief and find a comfortable place to express it. By facing our emotions and dealing with our grief, we can be present and help our children face their emotions and deal with their grief. One day at a time, just as it comes and whatever it brings. We can be ready.

CHAPTER 3

The C.O.U.R.A.G.E. Process

"Courage doesn't always roar. Sometimes courage
is the silent voice at the end of the day that says,
'I will try again tomorrow.'"
– Mary Anne Radmacher

I t takes courage, patience, wisdom, and hope to navigate the unpredictable waves of emotions that come during the grieving process. I like the Merriam-Webster definition of courage: "the mental or moral strength to venture, persevere, and withstand danger, fear, or difficulty." As I look back on my journey with grief and mourning after losing my husband and raising my children, I realize that it took courage from within myself to manage the storms of grief and be ready for the waves as they came crashing down. Being courageous is accepting your reality, being able to face your real emotions, and being brave enough to continue moving forward with your life.

Through my grief journey, there have been several strategies that I have used and learned from to help me navigate and learn to live again through my grief. They have evolved into a seven-step process that I call "The C.O.U.R.A.G.E. Process" to help navigate the journey of grief. Remember, the journey through grief is different for each of us. We all grieve differently and in our own time. I can tell you that "The C.O.U.R.A.G.E. Process" will help you accept where you are, face the emotions of grief, and, through the process, get through each wave as they come in no particular order.

The root of the word courage is *cor*, the Latin word for heart. Courage is a heart word. In one of its earliest definitions, the word courage meant "To speak one's mind by telling all from one's heart." As a society we typically associate courage with heroic and brave deeds. Courage is that inner strength and gaining that level of commitment required for us to speak honestly and openly about who we are and about our experiences, both good and bad. By doing this we can allow our hearts to start to heal from the pain or trauma of a loss. The ability to be courageous develops over time and includes efforts to fully accept reality, problem solve based on discernment, and push beyond ongoing struggles.

Nothing can or could have prepared you for the loss or for what your life will be now. It takes courage to grieve, to honor the pain we carry from the loss of a loved one. We can grieve in tears or in meditative silence. We can grieve in prayer or in song. We are individuals and we each grieve in our own unique way. In recognizing and feeling the pain of recent and long-held griefs, we come face-to-face with our genuine human vulnerability, with helplessness and hopelessness. These are the storm clouds of the heart that bring the waves of grief, but also bring the sunshine after the storm to calm the seas.

In these next few pages I want to introduce you to the C.O.U.R.A.G.E. process of healing along your grief journey. The road is not easy, and it will seem never-ending, but if you have the courage to take the first step, even if it is a tiny step, you can begin to heal your broken heart and tackle the enormous task of raising your children alone one day at a time. We can't snap our fingers and make everything be okay (oh, how I wish we could). Instead, it is a daily choice to survive and keep going in our grief journey.

The "**C**" in the C.O.U.R.A.G.E. process of healing through grief is to *create* space to grieve. You may be thinking, "I am already grieving, it is constant, and never goes away." Yes, that is true, but creating space for you to grieve and heal in a healthy way will help you heal on a much deeper level inside, at the heart level. This is the time to schedule activities in your calendar to remember to take care of yourself, to breathe, exercise, meditate, or take a long walk. Do something for you. You can't help anyone else (including your children) deal with their grief if you are not taking the time to grieve and help yourself. This is a really hard task for moms. I had a tough time with this, and I still do from time to time.

The "**O**" in the C.O.U.R.A.G.E. process is to *organize* your life. When we talk about organizing our lives, we think of keeping the house organized and tidy. But, in the case of grieving, being mentally and physically organized will aid in the healing process. Being organized means having structure for both you and your children. Having structure means you don't have to make as many decisions each day when your brain is foggy from grief.

The "**U**" in the C.O.U.R.A.G.E. process is to *understand* that grief is a process and that you are not alone. Understanding that grief takes time and there is no timetable to complete it will help you along the journey. Just because you are not where you thought you would be or where others think you should be by a certain time does not mean you are a failure. Grief does not have a set of rules that we follow and get through it. As we talked about earlier, grief is unpredictable like the ocean. We never know when a storm will come and waves of emotions will crash down on us.

The "**R**" in the C.O.U.R.A.G.E. process is *remembering* your loved one and *reflecting* on your life together. I don't want you to live in the past, because that is not healthy, but I do want you to take some time to remember and reflect on the life you had with your spouse. Remember all the good times you spent together and with the children as a family. This is going to be hard, but I believe it is necessary for healing to take place.

The "**A**" in the C.O.U.R.A.G.E. process is to *accept* the reality of the situation and where you are along your grief journey. Once we get to the point in our journey through grief where we can accept the reality that our spouse is no longer with us in their physical body, but they will always be with us in our hearts, then we can begin to feel a little glimmer of peace.

The "**G**" in the C.O.U.R.A.G.E. process is to be *grateful* as you move along your grief path and raise your children. I know what you are thinking. *How can I be grateful for losing someone I loved so much, when the pain is so intense?* Well, that is a good question and one I struggled with for many years.

The "**E**" in the C.O.U.R.A.G.E. process is to feel the *emotions*, recognize them when they come, and heal through the pain. Remember that analogy of grief being like an ocean with waves of emotions like fear, anger, sadness, guilt, disappointment, and shame that can come at any time and in no order. If we are to move forward through our grief, we must feel these emotions and face each one with the courage and determination to come out a better person because of the pain.

The C.O.U.R.A.G.E. process of healing through your grief is designed to break down each part of grieving and focus on it until we can begin to grieve and heal in a healthy way. One important thing to remember here is that the waves or stages of grief do not come in any certain order or timeframe. I designed this program to be used as a guide to help you move through grief in whatever stage you are at. You can reflect when it feels necessary. You should feel the emotions as they are coming and face them head on to get through to the other side and calmer waters. This book and the seven steps of the C.O.U.R.A.G.E process are meant to give you a place to start your healing journey and to help you along the way in whatever wave you are in at that time. You can refer at any time to whatever chapter resonates with you and your situation. I believe if we have the courage inside our hearts to go on and face our future, which is so uncertain, without our spouse we should make it the best we possibly can for us and our children. These practical seven steps in the C.O.U.R.A.G.E process are only a guide to assist you to learn to live again and find some joy and happiness along your grief journey.

CHAPTER 4:

Create Space to Grieve

*"It takes strength to make your way through grief,
to grab hold of life and let it pull you forward."*
– Patti Davis

Creating a space for grieving means not ignoring it and stuffing it down so you don't have to feel the pain like so many of us do to avoid the harsh reality. Holding space for grief with courage and self-compassion is something that takes time but is necessary for healing to begin and continue throughout the grief journey. Don't lose heart when you grieve; every human being grieves in their own way and in their own time. Don't try to force yourself to grieve. It will come at its own natural pace. Creating a space to grieve means being ready when it comes.

When I talk about creating space to grieve, I am talking about giving yourself time to grieve. Allow yourself time to process what has happened. If possible, if you work outside the home, take some time off work to get your thoughts together and get through the funeral or memorial service to say goodbye to your spouse. While I don't follow the stages of grief as they are laid out in a linear format, I do believe that anger, shock, and denial are some of the first emotions we face when we suffer a loss.

I can't say enough about how important having good self-care is during the grieving process. When we are in the middle of the storm we don't sleep, eat, or take care of ourselves very well because we are in a fog that makes us feel disoriented and confused. If you have to, write down what you are going to do in advance. For example, write "I will take the first hour in the morning for prayer and meditation" on your calendar if you are having trouble remembering to do those things. I know for me, if I don't write it on the calendar, I will not do it. Putting a task on your calendar holds that space for you to do that activity. It can be a task as simple as taking the dog for a walk, getting a massage, taking a bath, doing yoga, meditating, or telling yourself to slow down and remember to eat and breathe. You may laugh and say that those are things that you always do, and that you will remember to do them, but in the middle of grief the smallest of tasks can seem like mountains to climb.

As a mom, not only do you need to create space for yourself to grieve, but you also must create space for your children to grieve. Our children are different from us and their grief process will be different from ours. More than likely they will need your help along their journey through the grieving process and you must be willing to take the time to be there for them when they need you. A mom feels her children's pain and understands their grief in a way no one else in the world is able to. It takes courage to step up and be willing to hold space for your children to grieve, but it is necessary if they are to heal and move forward. Find ways to spend quality time with your children and consider doing things like painting, woodworking, pottery, or a creative activity that helps to get the feeling out into the space through creativity. This helps us to feel our way through the feelings and aid in the healing process. Even activities such as taking a walk together or having a date night for dinner with your children can create space for them to talk to you about their feelings and work through them together. If you have more than one child, it may be helpful to schedule one-on-one time with each one to give each child the opportunity to grieve with your help. Each child, just like each of us, will grieve in their own way and on their own time. Be there when they need you and schedule time to spend with each of them to give them the space to grieve with you there to love them through it.

I remember my children writing letters to their dad when they missed him or when they needed to release emotions they were feeling. I still have some of those letters, and they mean so much to me. I encouraged my children to talk to their dad when they prayed as if he was there with them and tell him whatever was on their mind if they did not want to talk to me about it. I always told my children that they could talk to me about anything. I wanted to know what they were feeling so we could address it and heal it to move forward.

When we can hold a space for grief and for it to be whatever happens and whatever it becomes, it allows us to wholeheartedly face it courageously and gives us a way to keep living. If we allow ourselves to feel the unpredictable, raw, intense pain of grief, to ride the waves and stay afloat in the raging sea of emotions that come, we can move forward. That doesn't mean that we forget, we just learn to live while we are in the middle of the storm and eventually the seas calm and we can take a breath.

One way I was able to connect with myself and my grief was through scrapbooking. I created time to work on a scrapbook highlighting Chris's military career as a Christmas gift for each of his brothers and his father so that they could remember and honor him. It made me feel good inside to be able to give them a gift that would mean so much to them, while helping me heal at the same time. When we try to think our way through grief, we often get stuck. We must feel our way through. Finding a creative way to release the feelings and deal with the pain of grief can be a great way to start the healing process.

Grief can manifest in our bodies as physical symptoms like chest pain, shortness of breath, insomnia, fatigue, weight loss or gain, and nausea, to name a few. It is important to recognize these physical symptoms of grief. This takes us back to taking the time for self-care and creating space to make sure we allow ourselves the time to eat, sleep, and exercise to combat some of the physical symptoms that come with the grieving process. When I speak of self-care, I mean creating the space and taking the time to care for ourselves during the grieving process. In the grips of grief, it is easy to forget to take care of ourselves, even on the most basic level, such as eating and sleeping.

However your grieving process shows up, it is important to be patient and let it unfold as it is supposed to for you. Remember there is no timeline for grief. We all grieve differently and in our own time. For some, after a few months it seems like they are better and moving forward with life; for others, like me, it takes years. Another aspect of self-care is not being too hard on yourself. You will make mistakes. You are vulnerable during the grieving process. Expect it, accept it, and move forward. If we can create the time and space to grieve, we can begin the healing process and start to put the pieces of our broken hearts back together again.

CHAPTER 5

Organize your Life

*"Only people who are capable of loving strongly
can also suffer great sorrow, but this same
necessity of loving serves to counteract
their grief and heals them."*
– Leo Tolstoy

Having a sense of organization in the middle of a chaotic situation can be challenging for most people. For young widows, now single moms, organization can be one of the only things that helps you get through each day and keep going. Being organized in your grief journey takes some practice and, if you were not organized before your loss, it can be difficult to suddenly just get organized.

Being organized means more than having all your bills and important paperwork in file folders in your filing cabinet. Yes, that is important, and it should be done. There are professional organizers who specialize in grief-induced clutter and can assist with organizing the important documents that will be needed in the months to come following the death of a spouse. The legal paperwork and financial documents such as life insurance and getting things changed over into your name should be done by a professional. In the early months of grief, the mind is foggy, and it is best to seek the help of a professional to make decisions that are important and will have lasting implications on your life and your children's lives.

Being organized means taking the techniques of creating space to grieve and putting them into practice –things like putting your tasks on a calendar and scheduling self-care time in your day or keeping yourself and your children on a routine. It is a little easier to keep a routine if your children attend school or if you must work during the day. At least you know that part of the day will be accounted for, so you only need to plan and manage the time on your calendar when you are at home. Honestly, for me, home seemed like the last place I wanted to be after Chris died. When I was home, I was surrounded by reminders of what I had lost.

I had to work outside the home before and after my husband died, so working was not a new concept for me. It was an outlet for me to go to work and take care of my patients because I felt like I was making a difference in someone else's life. It made my pain less when I was helping other people. I realize now that I worked all the time and that was a coping mechanism. I had subconsciously filled my work schedule to keep my mind busy so I would not have time to grieve or think about my own life. That is not the kind of organization I want you to consider as you plan your life while going through the grief process.

According to grief experts and psychologists, grief-induced clutter, or having an attachment to your spouse's belongings and not being able to part with them, can be normal in the early months following the loss. But if the grief-induced clutter and attachment to their belongings continues for a long period of time, it can be a sign that you never accepted the loss and you are stuck in your grief and not moving forward.

Organizing your home may include going through and organizing your spouse's belongings. This can be difficult because it will bring up or trigger some very strong emotions that will have to be dealt with as you decide what you will do with their belongings. But I believe that it helps you along the grieving process to face those emotions, feel them, and heal through the process. For years (and even today) I still cry when I am looking for something and I find something that belonged to Chris that triggers an emotion in me.

For me, organizing Chris's belongings was a healing project that I felt like I needed to do to have some sort of closure to help me start to heal the gaping hole that was left in my heart. Having children can make this task even more difficult, deciding whether to give away or keep some of the items for them to have later. I was able to give away some of Chris's clothes to a family that had lost everything, but most of his military and personal treasures I kept for Brianna and Dante to have to remember their daddy. Separating and storing them in bins or totes is one way to organize their belongings and it makes it easier for the children to go through their things and decide if they want to keep them later when they are ready.

There are different schools of thought about grieving and when the right time is to go through your spouse's belongings. I would say that it is an individual decision, and it depends on each person's journey through grief. For some, it is better to do it right away and get it over with, so that you do not have to see the constant reminders that your spouse is not there. But others can't find the courage or strength to get rid of anything or change anything and the house, car, and closet are kept just the way they were on the day they died. They feel as though they are throwing their loved one away by getting rid of their belongings. I am not saying that either way is right or wrong; it is what is right for you at that time on your grieving journey.

I know for me, getting Chris's belongings in order was a priority so I could start to heal. I needed to put things away in order to start letting myself move forward in the process. I was having such a hard time letting go, but getting his belongings organized for my children made me feel like I had made some progress, even if it was small. I know that not everyone has obsessive compulsive disorder and must have everything in its place like I do, but from what I have been told from others who I have helped along this journey, it was a sort of release to get their belongings organized. It helps to clear the mind in some way. Our mind during grief already feels like we have no control, but getting organized in some way gives us a sense of accomplishment and releases the feel-good hormones that make us feel better. Again, small steps of healing along our grief journey.

One person said it was rewarding and satisfying to give away some of her husband's belongings to others in need because she knew that is what he would have wanted. She said it gave her a sense of peace, made her feel good, and helped aid in the healing process at the same time. She said, "What good am I doing by keeping his clothes in the closet when someone out there needs them and I can help them by donating them to charity?"

I truly feel that organizing our outer world helps to organize our inner world and vice versa. And in the midst of grief, anything we can do to help keep our minds clear of extra clutter, like getting our house and life organized, will help us along our healing journey. So, having a schedule on our calendar and keeping our house organized are small but important things we can do to make life easier along our grief journey. After all, those are things we don't have to think about because they are already done. And, believe me, when you are in the middle of a storm and the waves are crashing down on you, the last thing you want do is make any unnecessary decisions. If it is written and scheduled on your calendar, the decision is already made, and you can weather the storm a little more easily for that day. Remember, we all have the same twenty-four hours in a day. It is what we decide to do with them that makes the difference in our lives.

CHAPTER 6:

Understanding Where You Are on Your Grief Journey

"Grief manifests in the realm of the soul, and although you may not be aware of it, you already have established mindsets regarding loss and grief."
– Devra Davis

I will refer to the stages of grief throughout this book as states of being so we can recognize them when we are feeling them, so we can grow and begin to heal. Even though there is no timeline in grief, the stages that Elisabeth Kübler-Ross wrote about are real and most of us will feel all of them at some point along our grief journey. The key is to understand what they are (denial, anger, bargaining, depression, and acceptance), and recognize them, in no certain order, when they come. By knowing what to expect we can be better prepared to deal with it. We are in uncharted waters where we have never been before and having a life preserver to hold onto can keep us afloat when we feel like we are drowning in our emotions.

In the early days and months of the grief process it is difficult to begin to understand what feelings and emotions will come up and when. It is hard enough to get through each day, much less look at six or twelve months down the road. As discussed in earlier chapters, grief does not have a roadmap or a certain timeline it follows. When I talk about understanding where you are on your grief journey, I mean recognizing the feelings and emotions you are having at that time and sitting with those feelings and letting yourself experience them. That may look like going for a walk in the woods, taking a warm bath, going somewhere and crying if you need to, or meditating for fifteen to twenty minutes while you feel those feelings in your heart. To be honest I have tried all of these things to help me feel whatever emotions I am feeling to get past them, and I have found through the years that I always feel better. My favorites are to take a hot bath and relax for twenty to thirty minutes, or just take a walk to meditate and be in nature, but I have to admit that sometimes I cry, and that's okay. So, do whatever makes you feel better. Love on your children – I know I used to just grab one of my children and hug them for no reason and I felt so much better. Even though they were looking at me like I was crazy, I didn't care. I secretly think they got something out of our interaction (me loving on them) too, even if they didn't admit it.

Do something that helps to calm you. When we try to push our feelings down and ignore them, they just become bigger and bigger until we have to let them out in some way. For many people, grief that is bottled up inside causes the body to feel physical pain and in some cases, illnesses can derive from the stress and pain that are not released. Probably the most common illnesses I have seen in my grieving patients through the years are digestive issues and insomnia or trouble sleeping. When we grieve, our immune systems are working overtime and are being taxed at their maximum capacity in some cases. Each of us is born with our own DNA and our own set of coping mechanisms for how we deal with everything in our life, including how we grieve. Just because one person gets remarried within a year or sooner after the death of their spouse and another person never remarries does not make either person wrong.

Each person has their own unique experience with grief. As people experience the process of grief, they will move in and out of each phase more than once along their road to healing.

Grieving is a process that does not completely end; it evolves and becomes integrated into your life. Grieving is a normal part of life, and the more we express our grief and don't try to hide from it, the easier it becomes to manage. Understanding that we each have our own grief journey to walk and knowing where we are at any given time can help us to manage those waves when they come. For me (and it may be the same for you), my grief most of the time felt like overwhelming sadness and pain, mostly in my chest, because it hurt to even take a breath. I relate that to my heart being broken in a million pieces. Each time I felt the chest pain and I had to stop to recognize or understand in order to feel the emotions, I was somehow mending a small piece and putting it back together bit by bit. This is when I would go to a quiet place, like the bathroom if I was at work, or to my bedroom if I was at home, and sit for a few minutes, meditating or crying, and let myself feel and heal, even on the smallest scale. To be honest, I did this more times than I want to admit in the months following Chris's death. I really didn't realize it at the time but looking back I can see that it helped me tremendously along my grief journey. Letting it out and dealing with the emotions that were welling up inside me, and not pushing them down and suppressing them, was healing on some level.

With time we gain a sense of understanding, or knowing, when we feel certain emotions welling up inside of us. Those feelings become familiar and we can recognize them more easily with each episode we experience. It's okay to cry. Washington Irving said it best when he said, "There is a sacredness in tears. They are not the mark of weakness, but of power. They speak more eloquently than ten thousand tongues. They are the messengers of overwhelming grief, of deep contrition, and of unspeakable love." Remember, it is okay to cry and feel your emotions as they come, however they show up for you.

As we move through grief, especially the first year where we are experiencing important dates on the calendar like the first holiday season or the first anniversary without our spouse, it helps to understand the milestones and big life events that will be there forever as a reminder of your past life together. Remember along your journey that grief never ends, but it changes as we grow through our pain.

It's a passage, not a place to stay. Grieving is not a sign of weakness, nor a lack of faith. It is the price of love. Grief can be messy and confusing. We must try to understand the process in order to heal from it.

Understanding where you are in the grief process does not mean knowing when you are going to wake up happy or all better. It means being able to recognize when you need to cry, or go for a walk, take a bath, or meditate. It means being quiet and tuning into your body and mind and feeling the emotion, riding the wave, and coming out in calmer waters.

CHAPTER 7:

Remember and Reflect

"The risk of love is loss, and the price of loss is grief-but the pain of grief is only a shadow when compared with the pain of never risking love."
– Hilary Stanton Zunin

Y ou may be asking yourself why I put remembering and reflecting in the middle of my seven-step process to healing through your grief. Well, that is a good question and I will answer it like this. As I have said before, grieving is different for everyone and there is no roadmap or timetable. That is why these steps in the C.O.U.R.A.G.E. process can be used at any time during your grief journey. You can apply these tips for healing in whatever wave or stage of grief you are in. Only you know where you are at any given time. I believe remembering and reflecting can happen at any stage or time in our grief journey; therefore, it can be applied at any time it feels right for you. It has been over sixteen years and I still sit and reflect and remember things that Chris and I did together and with our children.

Now I am not saying it takes that long to be able to remember, reflect, and appreciate the time you had together. It can happen at any time along your journey and I think it is good to have those moments to remind your heart of the love you felt and shared with them. I remember several instances throughout my journey as a widow when I would be meditating and working through some emotions that had come up, and out of nowhere a memory would pop into my mind. Sometimes I would cry, and other times I would sit and smile, reflect, and feel the love we shared in my heart. I felt joy and peace during those moments of reflection and remembering. I can't say for sure if Chris was present with me during these moments to comfort me, but I would like to think that he was there. I feel like as long as we remember our spouses in our hearts, we will always have a connection with them.

Grief can make us question our life, our purpose, and why we are still here and our spouse and soul mate isn't. As we move through our lives without our spouse or loved one, we will spend a lot of time reflecting and remembering the past life that we had and mourning the life we never got to have with them. This can be extremely difficult for very young widows who had planned a future together and felt it suddenly taken away. I know I felt that way at the tender age of thirty when Chris died and I was left with our two children to raise alone. I felt robbed and cheated. We had so many plans and dreams for our future after we retired and our children were grown. Plans that will never come true. It can be difficult at times to reflect and remember the plans and dreams you had with your spouse, but it is also therapeutic to help you heal, and you may just get to carry out some of those plans with your children someday. Some people take vacations and do activities that were planned as a family to honor the person who died. Like I said, everyone grieves differently. That does not make it right or wrong, it just is.

Children tend to reflect and remember their parent who has died through pictures, especially if they were young when the parent died. That is how my son, Dante, remembered his daddy since he was only four years old the last time he saw him alive. Through the years he would look through old photos of himself with his daddy and talk about what was happening in the picture. Later, as time passed, I asked him if he truly remembered his daddy and he said not really. It broke my heart for him to say that, but I knew that Chris had been gone from home for most of his young life.

Remembering the past and the happiness we had with our spouse can help us move forward in our grief journey. Journaling and writing down your feelings as you remember your spouse or loved one can be a very healing practice that you can do every day to help you reflect on your life. For many years I thought that if I stopped hurting or grieving, I would forget Chris, and I didn't want to ever forget him.

I have talked to other widows who have made vision boards remembering and reflecting on the time they spent with their spouse. The idea is to find pictures of you and your spouse and paste them on a poster board and hang it on the wall to look at every day as a reminder of your past life with them. It is but one way to reflect on your time spent with them and sit with the emotions that come, getting through each one as they come. Reflecting and remembering is healing. It gives us the hope to move forward in our life and appreciate the moments spent together even though we will long for even one more day with them.

Another way to remember our spouse or loved one is to write a letter to them, thanking them for all the wonderful memories you shared and how you will tell your children the stories so they can remember too. As moms who have children who are grieving the loss of their fathers, we sometimes feel like we are falling short and not helping them enough along their grief journey. It can be very therapeutic to have your children write a letter to their father and say whatever they want or need to say to heal some of the emotions they are feeling.

Young widowed moms get so caught up in their own grief while being the head of the household, struggling, and providing for their children that they forget to slow down and remember that their children are grieving too. One thing I learned the hard way through the years is that my children didn't care how much I bought for them or tried to give them the best of everything. What they wanted most from me was my time. They wanted to spend time with me, and I was so busy working and providing what I thought they wanted that I missed some of the most important moments in their childhood. I live with regrets and wish I could go back and do it over again, but I can't. So, not only do we need to remember our spouse and reflect to grieve and heal, we also need to remember that our children need our attention and help, and we can't be there if we are working and gone from home.

I have to say that my children and I have been very blessed to be a part of several memorials that have been built or renamed in honor of Chris. As I mentioned earlier, he was a Combat Controller in the Air Force Special Forces and he was loved and admired by all who knew him. I received a flag that had been flown over Afghanistan on a mission in honor of Chris. All the airmen on the mission signed it. I was also given a large framed picture of an airstrip in Afghanistan. The Combat Control Team had jumped in and taken over the airstrip and renamed it Matero Field. I was honored and humbled to see the great impact that he had on everyone who knew him. I remember and reflect on our great love when I look at those mementos and smile with joy that he was my husband and the father to my children. I was so blessed; the bad part is I don't think I realized it when he was alive. I cherish the memories I remember and reflect on at a deeper level now, a healing level. Remembering our spouses can be a very emotional healing experience if we allow it to be.

Through the years my children and I were contacted to come to the open houses of several events to honor Chris. The Combat Control School at Pope Air Force Base in Fayetteville, North Carolina, built a new road going to the school and they named it Matero Drive in honor of him. Another time we were asked to participate in the ribbon cutting ceremony at Keesler Air Force Base in Biloxi, Mississippi, to open a new training building they named Matero Hall. Of course, the kids and I went to both events and cut the ribbon. It was quite an honor, but as you can imagine the memories came flooding back and I spent many nights remembering and reflecting again on just what an amazing husband and father he had been. He was a true hero and that is how he will be remembered.

The reality for me was that Chris spent more time with his teammates and squadron than he did with me and the kids. I struggled with this emotionally for some time. Dealing with anger that came with the emotions was the hard part. But, as I said before, the grieving process does not come in a certain order. As I was remembering and reflecting on our life together, I realized that his military career was separate from the life he had at home with us. Remembering him as the person he was with us helped me to move past the anger and heal some of those emotions. My prayer for you is that you can heal through remembering and reflecting on your life with your spouse.

CHAPTER 8

Acceptance of What Is Now

"Most people move though grief at their own unique pace and many eventually find a peaceful acceptance. This does not mean that this terrible loss is "OK" but rather that one is no longer battling reality and has come to a place of acceptance of what is."

–M. Barns

A ccepting that our life will never be the same after losing our spouse and moving forward each day, putting one foot in front of the other, takes courage, strength, and determination that we did not know we had. Throughout this book I have discussed the stages of grief.

Although grief does not come in a certain order or time-frame, I do feel that we often experience all of these phases at some point in our grief journey. So, you may be thinking, why is acceptance not at the end of the C.O.U.R.A.G.E process for dealing with grief? Well, because during your grief journey, you will be faced with many changes that you will have to accept in order to move forward and heal. That may sound mean or cold-hearted, but it is unfortunately a fact that we all face at many times along our grief journeys. As I mentioned earlier in this book, the steps of the C.O.U.R.A.G.E. process will be interchangeable, and some will be happening at the same time at some point in your journey to healing and moving forward in your life.

"Acceptance" is one of those words used by the experts to describe a place you eventually get to along your grief journey. I don't believe the acceptance of my loss was the ending to my grief, but rather the portal to living more life as I continue along my grief journey. When I finally accepted my loss and that Chris was not coming home, I began to embrace and step into my new life as a widow and single mom. It was a life I did not ask for nor did I want, but one that I had to step into and learn to live again through the storms of grief, while raising my children alone. Accepting the reality of a situation does not dismiss the pain of the loss, it gives us a new pathway to travel. Accepting the life you have now been given can lead to the self-discovery of who we were meant to be. You may be thinking, "I don't care about self-discovery!" and I can relate. But I will tell you that if I had not been given this most difficult grief journey to walk and struggle through while raising my children alone, I could not have helped others along their journey. I look back now at who I was in 2002 when Chris died and at who I have become, and I realize that I have such a love for life now that I didn't have then. I don't take my time I get to spend with my parents, my children, and my grandchildren for granted anymore. I would like to say that I didn't then either, but I was so young and focused on getting my education and working that I just assumed we had all the time in the world. I can see now that losing Chris was a lesson in growing, understanding, and taking time to enjoy life in whatever season we are in. Accepting where we are can help us to move forward to where we are going, and it will help us to appreciate our new path even more after having to muster up the courage to face the struggles and heal our broken hearts along our grief journey. Accepting is taking things one piece at a time and mending our broken hearts to be whole again, so we can live again.

I have looked to the Serenity Prayer, written by Reinhold Niebuhr, to gain some clarity and find peace in my mind when I have felt lost or confused throughout my grief journey. Most of us remember the first verse of the prayer, which gives hope in times of despair, but I have included the entire prayer as a reminder that hardships such as losing a spouse and enduring the pain of grief can lead us down a pathway to find peace if we choose to accept and move forward through it.

> *God grant me the Serenity*
> *To accept the things I cannot change,*
> *Courage to change the things I can,*
> *And the Wisdom to know the difference.*

> *Living one day at a time,*
> *Enjoying one moment at a time.*
> *Accepting hardship as a pathway to peace,*
> *Taking, as he did, this sinful world as it is,*
> *Not as I would like it.*

Trusting that he will make all things right,
If I surrender to his will.
That I may be reasonably happy in this world
And supremely happy in the next.

The words of that prayer have so much depth and meaning when you really stop and think about it. I was mad at God for a long time after Chris died. I was angry that my life had been taken away, or so I thought. I was sad for my children to grow up without a father. Before I was able to accept the reality and move forward, I had to get through the anger and resentment I had built up inside. I was also mad at Chris for leaving me, as if he had a choice. We had finally gotten our lives together and we were settled. We had made it to where we wanted to be in life and *BAM,* it all changed in the blink of an eye. One split second in time and my life and the lives of my children were forever changed. I thank God every day that I decided to stay and had the courage to ride the waves of grief and come out a better person on the other side.

I want you to know that acceptance of the loss does not mean you are forgetting your spouse or their memory, or that you won't still grieve. It is a small stepping stone along the journey to help you move through your grief and be able to move forward to brighter days and calmer seas. I have realized through the years on my grief journey that if I try to ignore the facts that are before me or just not think about the pain, it causes me more pain and I feel stuck. By letting yourself accept and face what is, the pain, the loss, the uncertain changes to come, the awkwardness, the reality of being a single parent, you can start to see the path before you and, even though it is not certain, it is worth living.

Trust me, I fought it for a long time, but when I finally figured it out and I accepted what my life and my children's lives were going to be like without Chris, it made it more bearable, even on the hard days when the waves of grief came again. The reality is that we can't change our situation and bring our spouses or loved ones back. Believe me, if I could I would have for my children's sake and mine. I can't tell you how many times those words came out of my mouth when I was crying and holding one of my children and comforting them through a wave of grief. The heartache and pain I felt for them cannot be expressed in words. For me, accepting the fact that my children had to grow up without their father was more painful than the fact that I had to live without my husband. You will notice I did not say it was easy. I said acceptance is necessary in order to move forward to heal through our grief.

CHAPTER 9:

Gratitude along the Grief Journey

"Grief can be the garden of compassion. If you keep your heart open through everything, your pain can become your greatest ally in your life's search for love and wisdom."
– Rumi

Grief and gratitude are not usually thought of together, but they walk together. The insight that grief ultimately delivers is the gratitude for the time we have with the people we care about, and the gratitude we can develop about the natural cycle of life. That natural cycle is good and bad, joyous and sad, birth and death. Without the darkness, there is no light. We would not know we were in illumination if it did not leave us at times. Going through the grief journey does make us appreciate and be grateful for what we have now, knowing that what we lost is never coming back.

Grief changes over time, and as it changes, so then we change. Gratitude is realizing and noticing all the great things in your life, both past and present. The depth that you feel sorrow will be the depth that you will feel joy again. It may seem like an impossible task to ever feel grateful along the path of your grief journey, but if we can find something each day to be grateful for, our lives can begin to follow a new path. If you have ever heard anyone say, "have an attitude of gratitude," you may have wondered, what does that mean? Feeling gratitude is when you see your kids happy again, and that makes you happy. Feeling gratitude is being out with your friends and finding yourself smiling and laughing.

Having gratitude, accepting, and moving through your grief may bring the possibility of finding love again. The fear, sadness, and anger lessen, and you try to look at life in a positive way – with gratitude. You will never forget losing the person you loved more than anything. In the end, it is love that allows us to feel grief; it is loss that allows us to treasure what we have now, and what we've had before. It is in loss that we find peace again – and loss makes us and our experiences whole. It is not easy, but if you are able to find some gratitude along your journey at some point, you will find a way to create a new life for yourself.

None of us get to close the book on grief and forget the story. The story will stay with us and there will be times when we will relive the sadness, anger, pain, and longing contained throughout our grief journey. But, with a little gratitude, our journey will feel a little more colorful, a little more hopeful, and a little more optimistic about the future. It is not sad in and of itself that our loved ones die, it is sad that we lose them. We are sad for the loss we feel, and that loss is a constant reminder of the lives we shared together and that we were grateful for their presence in our lives. This can be one of the hardest phases or paths to walk in our journey through grief, but one of the most important in healing.

If you are struggling to find something to be grateful for, be grateful for a love so deep that you are a better person because of the great love you shared with your spouse. Appreciate the time you had with your spouse, and that he gave you beautiful children to remember him through. I remember that for the longest time every time I looked at my children, I saw Chris. After all, they both looked just like him and I could see him in them through their mannerisms and actions. At first in the early months after Chris died, I missed him so much that it hurt to look at our children because I would long to have him back with us. It took some time but eventually I embraced the fact that I had a part of Chris with me every day through our children. I felt grateful to see so much of him in our children and to see him live on inside them and through them, guiding and watching over them when I was not around. Yes, it took a long time, but I was able to eventually see how having gratitude for my time with Chris and our children would help me heal along my grief journey. I felt thankful that I had the time I had with him and that we were able to bring two amazing, beautiful children into this world. I began to be thankful and grateful for having loved so deeply and purely, because I realized that most people live their entire lives and never get the chance to experience what Chris and I had together.

We have a choice in our grief journey. We can either stay angry, bitter, and in pain, or we can choose to find a glimmer of hope and peace through finding something to be grateful for every day. You will be amazed at how good you feel when you decide to make that small but powerful shift in your thinking. I have found that journaling at night helps me to reflect on my day and write down what I am grateful for in my life. I have to admit, at first it was not easy because my heart was broken and I was still hurting so badly that I struggled to find things to be grateful for each day. I am here to tell you that it is possible to live through the grief and come out on the other side stronger and more courageous than you were before. It is possible to learn to live again after losing your spouse, and it is possible to raise amazing children even in the face of grief. Having a grateful heart will help heal your broken heart, one piece at a time.

CHAPTER 10:

Emotional Awareness

*"Although grief is painful, we can experience it
as a positive, life-changing journey. We can heal
from our devastation, shock, fear, and despair, and
return to life again, only this time more fiercely,
vulnerably, and wholeheartedly – more connected
to the love that surrounds us."*
– Eleora Han

We must feel our emotions in order to heal our emotions. One day at a time. We are all given the same twenty-four hours in a day; what we decide to do with it is up to us. That goes for dealing with the waves, peaks, and valleys of living through grief and taking things one day at a time. I know for me in my grief journey that some days it seems like a struggle to get through it minute by minute. I have learned that you can't go around, over, or under the emotions and feelings that come with grief; you must go through them, feeling and healing the emotions and coming out on the other side of the storm to calmer waters. And once you do that you will feel a little better. I want you to understand that you will move in and out of each phase or wave of grief more than once along this journey. The key is to be ready when the emotions and feelings come and face them head on, knowing that we are strong and courageous and we will get through to the other side and move forward a better person because we didn't give up in the face of adversity.

Walking along our path and experiencing each emotion is normal and a necessary, natural process of grieving. For example, when you are feeling sad that is an indication to take the time to slow down and look inward and ask God to heal your broken heart. It is through the experience of looking inward and re-evaluating our own life, feeling those emotions, even when painful, that the growth and learning occur. As you deal with each emotion, a valuable learning comes from each emotional struggle as well as a little bit of healing, whether we realize it or not.

Because of the intense pain and feelings of despair, we expect and hope that others who are close to us can fix it, comfort us, and make it go away. But grief is an individual process and it is very difficult for our loved ones who are also grieving and in pain to reach out and comfort us, even though we need it. It is important to remember that you cannot take any shortcuts as you deal with your grief and that each person's timetable is different. Ask for help when you need it. Your family and friends want to help but they do not know what to do or say to make you feel better.

I remember saying to my mom, who came to stay with me and the kids for a couple of months after Chris died, that everything is okay when everyone is around and you are surrounded by people who love you. It's after the funeral or the memorial service, when everyone goes home and you are alone, that you start to realize you miss the hugs. I missed the heartfelt hugs, the touch of another person. But most of all, I missed Chris.

My mom put her life on hold for me and my children for two and a half months to help me and for that I am eternally grateful. I think at this point I was still in shock and denial that my life had been turned upside down and I was trapped in a nightmare I could not wake up from. Looking back, I realize that during the early months and years after Chris died, I was not allowing myself to feel my emotions. I was in survival mode and I was just going through each day, dismissing my feelings and telling myself I should be in a better place than I was by now. Or I should be further along on my grief journey. I should feel better and have less pain by now. Through the years, I began to realize that we can't put a timeline on grieving. We can't just write out the phases of grief and check them off as we go through them. The analogy of the ocean and waves of grief that I talked about earlier in this book is the reality of the grief journey. The waves of grief will come and in no certain time or order. Let yourself feel the emotions as they come to begin the healing.

Having someone to talk to and express the feelings and emotions you are feeling at the time can be the difference between facing your grief and moving through it or staying in the emotion and letting it keep you stuck. Having a good support system is so helpful in aiding in the grief process. Having someone who can just take the kids for the evening, so we can sit with whatever emotion we are

feeling at the time and find a way through it is so important. You may notice that in the earlier steps of creating
space, understanding your emotions and allowing yourself
to feel them all work together to grieve through and heal
our broken hearts.

Allowing your children to feel their emotions and
taking the time to sit and listen to them and let them express
what they are feeling to you is so healing for them. You
may just think it is just talking, and maybe it is, but it can be
just what your children need to help them along their own
grief journey to healing. Our children do not always know
what they need, so it is our job as their moms to be mindful
of how they are feeling and pay attention to their behaviors
and how they communicate. These subtle observations can
give us clues as to how they are feeling. That is our chance
to schedule a time to take a walk or do a craft they love
together so that they will feel comfortable and safe express-
ing their feelings to us.

Remember, it is okay to take time for yourself to grieve.
It is natural to grieve a loss, especially one so deep as losing
a spouse. I will caution you that at times it feels like turning
to drugs or alcohol to numb your pain is the answer. But I
assure you that it is not the answer and it will not move you

closer to healing. In fact, turning to external things to make us happy will not succeed in bringing happiness to any area of our life. Wow, did it take me some time to figure that one out. I have found that meditation helps me to quiet my mind and sit with my emotions so that I can grow and heal even if only a tiny bit on my grief journey. Nowadays the waves of grief and emotions are not as severe, the storms are not as intense, and they don't last as long. They still come (at my most vulnerable times, like when I was writing this book), but I am prepared, and I can feel when I am slipping. I catch myself and climb back up before I slide down again.

You can learn to live again as you go through your grief journey. You may want to consider speaking with a counselor or attending a single parent support group for young widows through your local church or community center. Sometimes just talking to someone who doesn't already know you is a relief, because it allows you to freely express yourself without the concern that being honest is going to cause others to worry about you even more. That is one reason I created the C.O.U.R.A.G.E. process. My eight-week online course allows us to look at each component of our grief journey and breaks it down into bite-sized pieces that we can manage. I think of this course as a safe place that creates space to heal through our grief. Remember, we must be willing to recognize the feelings and emotions, to be able to feel them, to be able to heal them.

CHAPTER 11:

Obstacles We Encounter

*"What is the difference between an obstacle
and an opportunity? Our attitude toward it.
Every opportunity has a difficulty,
and every difficulty has an opportunity."*
— J. Sidlow Baxter

An obstacle is defined as a thing that prevents or hinders progress. If you read the above quote, then you know that with every season of life and every path we walk, there will be obstacles to face and overcome if we choose to. The journey you will walk through grief is no different and the same is true: you can either see the obstacles as impossible to get through and give up the fight or you can see the obstacles as an opportunity to grow as you conquer each one and move forward to a new life.

The obstacles that young, widowed, now single moms face are unique and can be life changing. I look back at my journey through grief and I am thankful that I had a career that afforded me the income to be able to raise my children and live a comfortable life. But for some young widows that is not the case. It is extremely difficult to raise children when your spouse was the head of the house and the sole income earner. It is during these times that we need to seek the help of our friends, family, and other resources to help us through.

Some of the obstacles I encountered along my grief journey raising my children included things like:

- Finding time for yourself when you are the head of the household, working, and raising children.
- Taking care of your children after coming home from work, cooking, cleaning, and helping with homework until it's time for bed. (If you were like me and your children slept in the bed with you, then you didn't have any downtime for yourself.)
- Comforting your children in moments of sadness and remembering/missing their father. (What do

you say in times like these?) Helping them to not lose faith when your faith is wavering at times.

- Trying to explain to your daughter why the schools have father/daughter dances and father/daughter sports banquets.
- Comforting my daughter at her wedding and standing in to dance with her because her father was not there for the bride/father dance.
- Trying to explain to my son about how a man is supposed to treat women when he has no one to look up to and learn from.
- How to get through the guilt and shame that comes with still being alive and feeling guilty for still living and maybe not wanting to.
- Having to make all the decisions by myself and wondering if I was making the right ones.
- During the early months after Chris's death, an obstacle that I faced daily was the fact that I felt angry at everyone for going on with their lives like nothing had happened. Didn't they know that my husband was dead and that my world stopped, and my heart was broken in a million pieces?

There are obstacles to anything in life that is worth living for and grieving the loss of a spouse is not different. I hate to admit it, but sometimes we are our biggest obstacle of all. I struggled with the feelings of not wanting to live and go on without Chris. Thoughts of suicide would come during my low periods, but I would remind myself that I had been given the most important job of my life and that was to raise our children. After all, they were babies. They depended on me. I did not want anyone else to suffer the way I was, and Lord knows I didn't want my children to suffer any more than they already were. I realized I had so much to live for and that I needed to overcome whatever obstacles came to raise my children.

My prayer is that no obstacle is too big that you can't face it and get through it. At times we struggle with wanting to try to tackle large projects all at once, like grief. We just try to rush through it to feel better. The reality is that grief can't be rushed. We must tackle one obstacle or emotion at a time and get through it. We might even have to slow down and take one piece at a time, or, like I said earlier, some days it's like one minute at a time, and that is enough. I am not saying that your grief journey will be impossible to navigate on your own. I am confident that you will get through it. I just know from experience that having a plan or steps to follow along the journey makes it a little easier to navigate and the obstacles that come seem a little more manageable because you are ready. The courage process gives you an easy to understand outline of how to manage the waves of grief as they come, and practical ways to get through them and learn to live again in your new life. We are still faced with the same obstacles to overcome. My hope is that by applying the steps and techniques in the C.O.U.R.A.G.E. process outlined in this book, you will be able to overcome them and move forward faster and easier than if you didn't apply these principles.

CHAPTER 12

You Are Not Alone in Your Grief Journey

"Deep grief sometimes is almost like a specific location, a coordinate on a map of time. When you are standing in that forest of sorrow, you cannot imagine that you could ever find your way to a better place. But if someone can assure you that they themselves have stood in that same place, and now have moved on, sometimes this will bring hope."
— Elizabeth Gilbert, Eat, Pray, Love

Do you know that many people give up on the journey through grief? They decide early on that they are meant to grieve forever, and they sit down in it and make a home in grief. Some people start with the hope that they will get through it, but as they experience waves of grief it knocks them down again and again, and then one day they just decide not to get up, give up trying to cope, and live in the pain. Moving through grief is not for the weak. It takes courage. It takes a willingness to confront the pain and emotions of grief along an unpredictable path. You can't tell me that doesn't take courage. If you are experiencing the extreme emotions of grief and you are still standing, then you are courageous. Pat yourself on the back for getting up and facing today and every day. If you have children to raise, find the courage you need and with the grace of God you get through one day at a time. Again, I want to commend you for staying in the fight and having the courage to keep pushing forward.

You see, there is a process in grieving, we just don't know what our process will be until we move through it in our own unique way and in our own time. The intensity of your grief is directly related to the strength of your attachment to what was lost. The greater the love, the greater the loss will feel. Everyone grieves differently. I can tell you that once I accepted the reality that Chris was gone and not coming home this time, I was able to fully be present with my children and made it my mission in life to raise my children and to help other young widows like me who woke up to a nightmare that they felt would never end. I am here to tell you that if you choose to be courageous and stand in your power and feel the emotions and waves of grief, to put on your life vest and swim when you need to and float when you can, you will get through the storms to find peace in calmer waters.

Throughout my grief journey I have read countless books on grieving. In my readings, I came across the writings of Gary Roe. In his book *Be Patient I'm Grieving*, he writes, "Loss is painful. It crushes hearts, steals dreams, and destroys relationships. Grief can be terribly lonely. Those who are grieving need us. They need you." Those words resonated with me in a way that I knew God was speaking to me and preparing me for my life's purpose, to help other widows along their broken hearted, unpredictable walk with grief and to learn to live again. The key to dealing with grief is to embrace it and to allow all the varying feelings of grief to flow. As discussed throughout this book, there is no timeline for grieving. It comes unexpectedly and is unpredictable, but one thing I know for sure is it will come. If you have lost your spouse, you will grieve. It is the body's way of healing. You can't ignore it or pretend that it is not happening, because one way or another it will show up.

If you feel like you are alone and you don't have a support system on your journey through grief, I am here to tell you that you are not alone and that there are thousands of other widows that are sitting on their beds, crying and trying to decide on what choices they are going to make as they walk the unpredictable, unrelenting, path of grief. I would like to offer you a path that is courageous and will help you move through those stages and waves of grief when they come and help you learn to live and find joy again while raising your children alone after losing your spouse. In my program we face our grief and look at it perhaps in a different way than the traditional methods I was taught in my medical training to deal with grief. The steps of the process are interchangeable and can be used whenever necessary to coincide with your current situation and emotions. My program is unique because there are no set-in-stone rules to follow. It is designed to meet you where you are on your grief journey and give you practical and proven guidelines to help you manage your grief more effectively and with less struggle along the way. I know because I have been where you are, I know the pain and heartache that you are feeling, and I have learned to live again in my grief and find joy and happiness I thought would never be possible after losing Chris. My course is an eight-week course that will transform your life and change the way you view your grief journey. You can check it out at www.thecourageprocess.com.

I will leave you with this quote by Elisabeth Kübler-Ross and John Kessler: "The reality is that you will grieve forever. You will not 'get over' the loss of a loved one; you will learn to live with it. You will heal, and you will rebuild yourself around the loss you have suffered. You will be whole again but, you will never be the same. Nor should you be the same, nor would you want to." You have a decision to make – are you going to move through your grief journey with courage or are you going to succumb to the grips of the pain and stay in your grief? For you and your children's sake I hope you choose to move forward with courage and to learn to live again.

Thank You

I want to personally thank you and commend you for having the courage to pick up this book and read it. That tells me that you are ready to hear what I have to tell you and you are looking for answers to all your questions surrounding your new life as a widow.

You were guided to picked up this book for a reason and I am so glad you did. My prayer is that through my seven step C.O.U.R.A.G.E process you will gain some sense of direction and clarity on your grief journey.

It is one thing to read the steps in this book, but it is another to apply these principals daily in our busy lives.

If you feel like you would like more guidance and someone to walk with you on your journey, please email me your information at <u>dr-roneisa@thecourageprocess.com</u> schedule a strategy session with me to see if I can help you.

During this strategy session call we will get to know one another and figure out where you are and if we are a good fit to work together.

Please visit my website at <u>www.thecourageprocess.com</u> to learn more about me and my eight-week transformational program to help you learn to grow and cope along your grief journey and learn to live again.

Looking forward to hearing from you,

Dr. Roneisa Matero

About the Author

Dr. Roneisa Matero is a veteran, nationally certified family nurse practitioner, grief expert, certified health and wellness coach, and a certified life coach, with over twenty-eight years of experience in helping and serving others. Roneisa joined the USAF in August 1990, just after graduating from high school. She spent five years as a flight medic serving her country. During that time, she was deployed to England, Italy, Turkey, and Saudi Arabia during the Gulf War before she took an early discharge in May 1995 to take care of her family and further her education as a registered nurse. Roneisa received her bachelor's degree as a registered nurse in 1997 from the University of Arkansas for Medical Sciences before having her second child a month later and moving to North Carolina.

She returned to college in September 1998 to pursue her master's degree in nursing as a Family Nurse Practitioner at Duke University and graduated with honors in May of 2000. In May 2014 she again returned to college to pursue her doctoral degree in nursing and graduated with honors from Maryville University and earning her Doctor of Nursing Practice degree in May 2016.

Roneisa has been widowed since August 7, 2002, and has immersed herself in raising her children and dealing with the loss of her husband and father to her children. She lost her husband, a Combat Controller in the Air Force, in a plane crash along with nine other United States Air Force service members.

Roneisa has been in the medical field and helping people for the past twenty-eight years. Her career gave her the means to go on and support and raise her children. During her journey through grief, she realized she wanted to help other widows with children survive the debilitating effects of grief while learning to live again and move forward in a positive way.

Roneisa has helped hundreds of people throughout the years to deal with various aspects of the grief process and the trials and tribulations associated with grieving the loss of a spouse. She has lived and experienced the grief and pain that come with losing a spouse and being left alone to raise the children. After her youngest child, Dante, got married and left home in 2016, she decided to give in to her long-time desire to write a book that would help widows with children cope with the grief and loss. She was inspired to write a book that she wished she had had all those years ago when her life was suddenly turned upside down and she was left to raise her two small children alone.

Roneisa lives in a small town in east Texas close to her children and grandchildren. She is an online adjunct professor for Abilene Christian University, Chamberlain University, and Walden University in the Doctor of Nursing practice programs, and she works part-time in the emergency department as a family nurse practitioner. She enjoys taking long walks along a beautiful beach or in the mountains to connect with nature, writing, and, most of all, spending quality time with her family and helping others any way she can.